THE PARADOX OF CHOICE

Why More Options Don't Always Mean More Happiness

Tips for Making Career Decisions

MICHAEL LAUREN

Copyright © 2024 Michael Lauren

All rights reserved. No part of this publication may be reproduced, distributed transmitted in any form or by any means, including photocopying, recording or other electronic or mechanical methods, without the prior written permission of the publisher, except in the case of brief quotations embodied in critical reviews and certain other noncommercial uses permitted by copyright law

DEDICATION

I dedicate this book to people whose hearts are burdened by the thought of endless possibilities and who stand on the edge of potential.

It might be a lamp in your chosen labyrinth, illuminating the tools you already have rather than providing the "right" path.

Because everyone of you has a complex map inside of you that is woven from your experiences, values, and innermost thoughts. Discover how to interpret this map, have faith in its compass, and dance with freedom's contradiction.

This book is an invitation to talk, not a guarantee of answers. It hints at the delight of accepting "enough," the paralyzing hold of FOMO, and the beauty and burden of choice.

Together, let's explore the landscapes of possibility as agents of our own destiny rather than as passive tourists. May every page serve as a brushstroke on the canvas of your life, a reminder that you are the one with the ability to make sensible decisions.

Therefore, dear reader, while you traverse the endless paradox of choice, take a bold step forward, embrace the dance of uncertainty, and allow this book to serve as your guide rather than your master.

ACKNOWLEDGMENTS

Without the bright minds that lighted my way, this book—which was born out of the tangled strands of the paradox of choice—would not have been possible. I want to thank each and every one of you:

To my inspiration, the contradiction itself: For the incessant queries you uttered, the debilitating "what if" mutterings that served as the catalyst for my investigation. You showed me the strength of indecision, the beauty of the path not taken, and the bravery required to make a decision at all.

To the foundations of knowledge: To the writers whose works served as stepping stones for me and whose wisdom helped me understand the difficulties of decision-making. To the scholars, thinkers, and storytellers who prepared the way for this investigation.

To my family, the steadfast hands that kept me afloat when the wave of uncertainty threatened to sweep me under: To my anchors in the storm. To my friends, the shoreline dotted with laughter, where I found inspiration and comfort. When I veered off course, your love, a steadfast light, led me back on course.

And to you, my reader: For following the lines of this word-woven tapestry, for stepping into this maze alongside me. My compass, your engagement, and my reward are your curiosity. I hope these pages inspire you to dance with paradoxes of your own and offer you the courage to follow your own path—your own "complete one."

Thank you from the bottom of my heart. You own this book just as much as I do.

TABLE OF CONTENT

THE MENTOR'S CORNER 1
WHY DOES THIS HAPPEN 4
PROGRESS >> ACTIONS 10
THE 5/5/5 RULE 14
COUNTERACT FOMO with JOMO 18
LOWER THE STAKES 23
YOU DON'T MAKE THE RIGHT DISCISION 25
CONCLUSION 28
Note 30
ABOUT THE AUTHOR 32

THE MENTOR'S CORNER

The topic of today's Mentor's Corner is decision-making, which is a crucial professional skill, especially when faced with a multitude of possibilities. Oddly enough, creating too many alternatives can cripple and destroy our life even though they are meant to free us. I'll tell you why and give you some of the methods I use to become "unstuck."

The awful decision paradox, ah. The feeling of being overwhelmed when faced with a plethora of options, all of which appear perfect yet prevent you from making a choice. Don't worry, young Padawans; The Mentor's Corner is here to help you navigate this modern labyrinth.

First, let's dispel the myth of the "perfect choice." It is a unicorn—a product of our arrogance. Every decision has subtleties and drawbacks of its own. Instead of aiming for perfection, embrace the dance of discovery. This is your chance to sample the diversity of life's flavors and dance with opportunity.

After that, silence your inner critic. That voice whispering, "What if I choose wrong?" is actually a saboteur in disguise. Keep in mind that every choice you make is a step toward a new experience, a new insight, or a new understanding. The most incredible adventures occur when you embrace the unknown.

Immediately arm yourself with knowledge. Analyze, compare, and refer to the experiences of your predecessors. However, remember that information excess is a quicksand trap. Establish limits, pick your sources wisely, and trust your instincts to help you navigate the deluge of information.

**Lastly, don't be afraid to act! The longer you ignore it, the more deeply the paralysis of analysis bites its nails. Choose with courage and a sense of adventure. Selecting a different option from the "perfect" one will help you develop, learn, and become closer to your goal than you were before.

Recall that the paradox of choice is a puzzle to be solved rather than a monster to be slain, Padawans. Accept the abundance, develop the ability to dance with ambiguity, and have faith that every decision—even the one that seems the most incorrect—leads to a better future. Now set out, and may you be guided

THE PARADOX OF CHOICE

by The Mentor's Corner's wisdom!

WHY DOES THIS HAPPEN

It was not too difficult to choose a career back then.

You didn't.

You followed in your family's footsteps or worked at the village's sole employment, and that was that. Because there were no "careers" to choose from, people rarely changed careers.

Regarding "career satisfaction," well.

You did what you had to do, that's all. You fed your family.

(Our predecessors pursued their occupations for so long that they acquired surnames, such as Smith, Fisher, Mason, and so forth.)

Although that sounds awful, the irony is...

They Were Not Probably Satisfied With Their Jobs Than We Are!!!!

Let's go back in time to the present and see the vast array of jobs that are available to us today:

You have the option to work as a teacher, content producer, influencer, business owner, or self-taught programmer with a focus on one of the 20 available programming languages.

Moreover, the bewildering array of educational opportunities—from part-time MBA programs to career-change schools to coding bootcamps and "externships"—

"Can I tell you about a few items that aren't on the menu?"

The result of all this choice?

We can't settle down and focus on a single career, we question ourselves all the time, and we're left with a nagging of :-

Cognitive Overload:

> An excessive amount of knowledge is beyond the capacity of our brains to process. We get overwhelmed when presented with a plethora of possibilities, each demanding examination and contrast. Decision fatigue results from this, which makes it more difficult to take in information and decide what to do.

Fear Of Missing Out (Fomo):

> An ongoing worry that we could pass up something better is fueled by the multitude of possibilities. We get unhappy and regretful when we compare our selected option to all of the unchosen ones because of FOMO.

Growing Expectations:

When we have more options, we become more demanding of the "perfect" solution. Because of this, it is more difficult to be fully content with any one decision because it is unlikely to live up to our inflated ideal.

Loss Aversion:

Our innate tendency is to put preventing losses ahead of pursuing gains. This means that we are further paralyzed in our uncertainty by the possible "loss" of all the unchosen possibilities, which looms larger in our minds than the potential benefit from the selected one.

Analysis Loop:

We become mired in a cycle of overanalyzing and comparing when we fall victim to the FOMO and loss aversion traps. We continue to look for "the perfect" solution, putting off enjoying the adventure and our true priorities.

The paradox of choice basically results from an

imbalance between our brains' limits and the abundance of possibilities available to us. We haven't evolved to deal with such a deluge of information and pressure to make decisions.

It's a recurring theme in the queries I receive as well, such as this one from a few days ago, which say's

"I could continue at my current employer and get promoted in two years, but I'm stuck. However, I'm experiencing some "boredom." For something more thrilling, I believe it would be nice to join a developing startup. Having said that, I may return to school to acquire a formal programming degree and change careers completely. Maybe I should just stay in my current position and find a more secure corporate position. Assistance?"

ULTIMATLY:

MORE CHOICE => MORE UNCERTAINTY

It's a real problem, so today I thought I'd offer up a few different perspectives that might help.

Let's go.

THE PARADOX OF CHOICE

PROGRESS >> ACTIONS

People are creatures of motion and stillness; they are attracted to both the excitement of forward motion and the coziness of motionlessness. This weaves a fascinating tension across our lives between action and inaction.

We often get stuck when faced with a choice and stress over making the best choice.

A better Option?

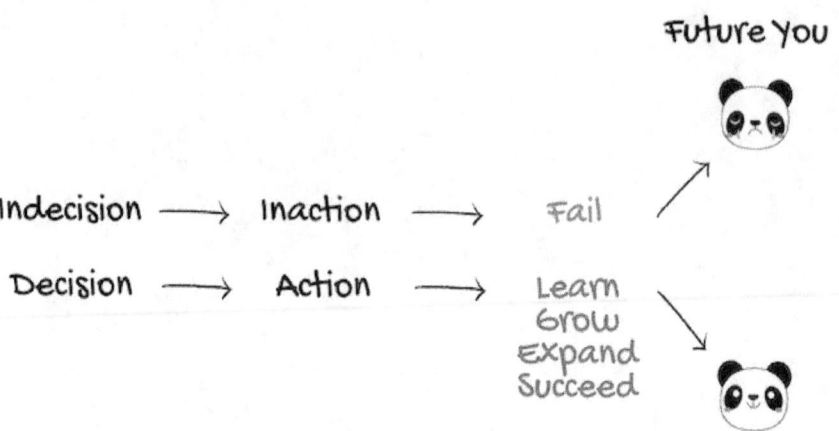

START TAKING ACTIONS DOWN ON ONE PATH:

Begin moving along a single route. Generally speaking, decisions are not always as final as we believe them to be; you can still change your mind later.

Afterall, which is preferable—testing out each alternative for three (3) months or trying to determine which is the greatest option while waiting six (6) months?

PROGRESS:

the insatiable need to create and progress, the never-ending march forward, and the quest of improvement. It involves scaling mountains, picking up new abilities, pushing limits, creating empires, and leaving traces in the sands of time. Progress is the journey of the hero, the victory of the underdog, the scientific discovery. The murmur of "what if?" and the fire that fires in our stomachs are what drive us onward.

INACTION

The stillness, the inhale, the silent thought in the middle of the flurry. It's letting go of the reins, enjoying a sunset, and listening to the wind rustling the leaves. A writer's incubation stage, an artist's blank canvas, and a monk's meditation are all characterized by inaction. It is the rich soil in which thoughts sprout, fears fade, and the soul is restored.

This dance between progress and inaction plays out in every facet of our lives:

- In our careers: We strive for promotions, chase deadlines, and build empires. But we also need time for reflection, for recalibration, for letting new ideas simmer.
- In our relationships: We nurture connections, navigate conflicts, and work towards understanding. But we also need space for

solitude, for introspection, for simply being present.

- In our personal growth: We learn new things, push our limits, and expand our horizons. But we also need time for rest, for integration, for letting new knowledge sink in.

THE 5/5/5 RULE

....

Citrus vs. cream cheese? Html or Css? Should I marry Jennifer or Mary? When faced with decisions big and small, I like the 5/5/5 rule:

Will this matter in 5 days? 5 months? Or 5 years?

This might help you understand the real weight of the decision and make it easier to choose. Often, many decisions we're 'stuck' on won't even matter in a few months, much less a few days. Recognizing that takes the pressure off.

Whether something matters in 5 days, 5 months, or 5 years within the context of the paradox of choice depends on the specific decision you're facing and the lens you choose to view it through. Here's how each perspective might play out:

5 days:

- **Short-term focus:** This lens prioritizes immediate consequences. If the decision has a clear and significant impact within 5 days, it might be easier to justify the effort of choosing. For example, choosing a restaurant for dinner tonight wouldn't hold much weight in 5 months or 5 years.

- **Pressure cooker:** The short timeline could exacerbate the paradox's effects. Feeling rushed to potential long-term consequences, but also requires some time to unfold, 5 months might be a relevant timeframe. For example, choosing a career path could have major impacts in 5 months (starting a new job) and even more in 5 years (career trajectory).

- **Deeper analysis**: The choose amidst many options could lead to decision fatigue and dissatisfaction.

5 months:

- **Medium-term perspective: This** lens balances immediate needs with future considerations. If the decision has

longer timeframe allows for more research, reflection, and consultation. This can help avoid impulsive decisions and increase confidence in the chosen option.

5 years:

- Long-term vision: This lens prioritizes the big picture and the ripple effects of choices. If the decision has potential lasting impacts on your life or others, 5 years might be a crucial timeframe to consider. For example, choosing a partner or a major life change might shape your life significantly in 5 years and beyond.

- Perspective shift: Taking a long-term view can help you detach from the immediate overwhelm and anxiety. It can remind you that even if the present choice feels daunting, it's a small step in a larger journey.

Ultimately, the question of "whether it matters" is subjective and depends on your values, priorities, and the specific decision at hand. The key takeaway is to approach the paradox of choice with a balanced perspective, considering both the immediate and future consequences of your options. By doing so, you can make choices that are aligned with your long-term goals and bring you deeper satisfaction.

COUNTERACT FOMO with JOMO

Accept the Joy of Missing Out instead of the Fear of Missing Out: the freeing realization that by selecting one path, you're releasing yourself from the drawbacks of the other options.

To put it another way... visually, sometimes the grass isn't always greener on the other side; instead, it's drier, less pristine, and covered in dog waste.

"I worry everyone's got FOMO but me."

The overpowering sensation that arises from the paradox of choice when presented with an infinite number of possibilities can quickly stoke FOMO (fear of missing out). The joy of missing out, or JOMO, is a potent counteragent, though. Let's examine how to accept JOMO and be happy with your decisions:

1. Modify your viewpoint:

- Transition from "missing out" to "choosing in": Honor the pathways you intentionally pick rather than lamenting the ones you didn't. Every decision is a chance to make a significant investment.

- Concentrate on the good: Consider the special advantages and experiences that come with following your chosen path rather than obsessing over what you could be missing.

2. Identify Your Top Priorities:

- Determine your true priorities by listing your beliefs, objectives, and aspirations. Your decisions will feel more gratifying if you align them with them, and the appeal of unchosen routes will be diminished.

- Develop your ability to say no: Don't be scared to turn down offers that conflict with your priorities. Rejecting one item makes room and energy for the things that really count.

3. Show appreciation:

- Spend some time appreciating what you have by thinking back on the experiences, chances, and blessings that come with following your chosen route. Having gratitude in your life makes you happier and less tempted to judge others by their lives.

- Honor modest victories: No matter how tiny, acknowledge and applaud your progress. This boosts your devotion to your chosen course and encourages pleasant feelings.

4. Adopt JOMO customs:

- Make "JOMO moments": Set aside time for pursuits that make you happy and fulfilled, regardless of approval from others or comparative analysis. This could include engaging in a hobby, reading, or going on a nature walk.

- Make connections with like-minded people: Be in the company of people who embrace your decisions and encourage you on your JOMO journey. Refrain from evaluating yourself against others who are always chasing the next big thing.

5. Know That It's A Journey, Not The Destination:

- Recognize that unchosen routes will always exist; try not to let the "what ifs" consume you. Accept the unknown and concentrate on living life to the fullest on this trip.

- Treat yourself with kindness: Recognize that JOMO is a practice rather than a perfection and forgive yourself for any moments of FOMO.

You can mitigate the detrimental impacts of FOMO and discover happiness and fulfillment in your decisions by deliberately fostering JOMO. Recall that the paradox of choice can be a liberating chance to find and accept your own route, rather than a bewildering labyrinth.

So, exhale deeply, be proud of your decisions, and revel in the happiness that comes with avoiding things that don't really fit with who you are. Recall that the most satisfying life is one that is led in joyous pursuit of your true passions rather than one that is measured in comparison to others.

LOWER THE STAKES

Making large, snap judgments that change our lives without considering all the options is where we frequently fall into difficulty.

To test the waters, I believe it would be wiser to develop tiny, low-stakes trials. In this manner, you can acquire the data you need to make a more informed decision without having to give it your all.

Suppose you are attempting to select a career.

Setting up a chat with an experienced professional in the field will enable you to determine whether or not you enjoy it more on a typical Tuesday than binge-watching a popular Netflix series or a YouTube advertisement.

One more instance:

You're considering changing careers to become a UX designer because you want to create user interfaces for businesses on the web and on mobile devices. However, you're not positive that you'll adore it.

You may try your hand at a low-risk endeavor like a freelance design assignment. Join freelance marketplaces like Fiverr or Upwork, set up an account, and take on a short 10-hour project for a cheap starting fee. Dealing with actual clients, deadlines, and issues will provide you a far sharper perspective than you would otherwise get.

"*I'm making a decision! Stop confusing me with facts!*"

YOU DON'T MAKE THE RIGHT DISCISION

....

"You don't make the right decision, you make the decision right," a mentor once advised me when I was having a terrible time choosing between two excellent options.

Though strange, it feels liberating. You can choose any option and do your best with it if there isn't a "perfect decision."

The paradox of choice isn't just about making the "right" decision. In fact, the concept of a universally "right" choice is often an illusion within this mental maze.

So, instead of obsessing over making the "right" decision, here's a different approach:

- Focus on making a good enough decision: Aim for a choice that meets your needs, aligns with your values, and allows you to move forward without debilitating regret.

- Embrace the "good process": Focus on gathering information, reflecting on your priorities, and making a decision with the best resources available at the time.
- Accept the uncertainty: There will always be unknowns. Learn to navigate uncertainty with confidence, knowing that every choice is a step on your journey.
- Trust your intuition: Sometimes, the best choice is the one that feels right in your gut. Don't discount your intuition in the face of overwhelming information.
- Learn from every choice: Every decision, good or bad, offers valuable lessons. Reflect on your experience and use it to inform future choices.

THE PARADOX OF CHOICE

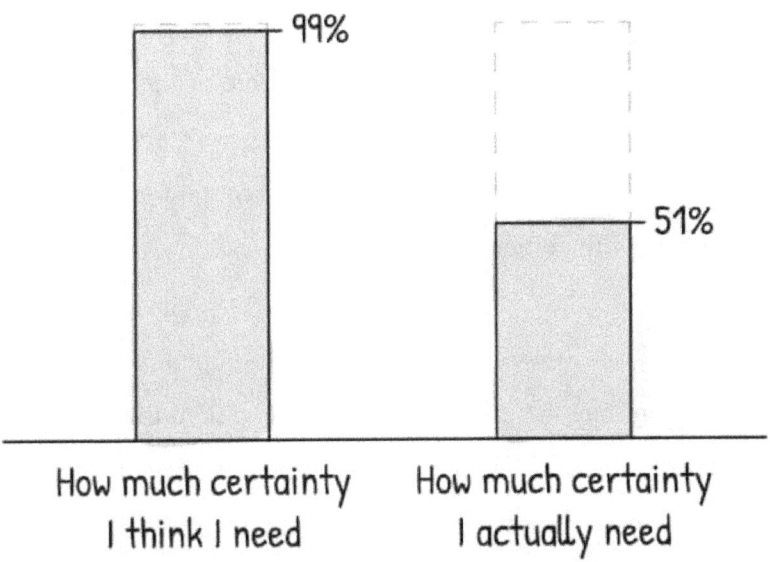

Remember, the paradox of choice isn't about finding the "right" answer. It's about navigating a complex landscape of possibilities with clarity, courage, and a willingness to learn and adapt. Embrace the journey, trust your own path, and make choices that move you closer to a life that feels authentic and fulfilling.

CONCLUSION

Standing at the precipice of the final page, it's tempting to offer a neat conclusion, a definitive answer to the riddle of the paradox of choice. But the journey, as we've discovered, isn't about finding "the answer." It's about the dance itself, the constant evolution of our relationship with choice.

So, instead of a tidy bow, let's leave the ending open, a whispered invitation to continue the pilgrimage. We've explored the seductive lure of endless options, the paralyzing grip of FOMO, and the liberating power of saying "no." We've learned to navigate the landscape of our values, to listen to the whispers of intuition, and to embrace the beauty of the "good enough."

But the dance doesn't stop here. The world, with its infinite possibilities, still pulsates around us. New choices will arise, new paradoxes will present themselves. And that's the essence of this journey: to not shy away from the complexity, but to embrace it.

Remember, the paradox of choice isn't a prison, it's a playground. It's an invitation to experiment, to explore, to create your own unique path through the vast landscape of possibilities. So step into the unknown with courage, trust your own compass, and let the dance of choice continue, one deliberate, joyful step at a time.

This isn't the end of the story, it's the beginning. It's the beginning of a life lived not by default, but by conscious, deliberate choice. The choice to be the architects of our own destinies, not merely passengers on a pre-determined route.

Go forth, dear reader, and choose. Choose the life you yearn for, the path that ignites your soul. Choose with courage, choose with wisdom, choose with joy. And as you do, remember, you are not alone in this dance. We are all travelers on this path, navigating the paradox together. Let us celebrate each other's choices, learn from each other's stumbles, and together, build a world where choosing isn't a burden, but a beautiful, exhilarating dance.

Note

The Problem: We live in a world overflowing with options, leading to a paralyzing fear of missing out (FOMO) and the overwhelming burden of choice. This is the paradox of choice.

The Solution: Shift your mindset from scarcity to abundance. Embrace the journey, not just the destination of your choices. Here are some key takeaways to guide you:

- Reframe your perspective: Instead of "missing out," focus on "choosing in." Celebrate the unique paths you choose, not the ones you don't.
- Clarify your priorities: Identify what truly matters to you. Align your choices with your values and goals to make them feel more fulfilling.
- Embrace JOMO (Joy of Missing Out): Learn to appreciate what you have and focus on experiences that bring you joy, independent of external validation.
- Lower the stakes: Start with smaller choices to build

confidence and trust your decision-making skills. Don't let every decision feel like life or death.

FINALLY

The paradox of choice is not about finding the "right" answer, it's about navigating the complexity of possibility with clarity, courage, and a willingness to learn and adapt. Embrace the dance of choice, and let it guide you toward a life that feels authentic and fulfilling.

Remember: These key takeaways are just a starting point. The

ABOUT THE AUTHOR

I'm Michael Lauren Six years ago, I found myself frustrated with the sea of misleading career advice online, so I started seeking for Alternative to navigate the Paradox of my Career. The goal was simple: provide guidance that actually works.

But some research were only the tip of the iceberg. There was a lot of clichéd, generic career advice out there. So, I started this write up, I talk about real career strategy, informed not only by my experiences but by my conversations with industry leaders, senior coaches who train CEOs, and people with way more experience than I have.

www.ingramcontent.com/pod-product-compliance
Lightning Source LLC
Chambersburg PA
CBHW070955220526
45471CB00007B/3037